In the tracks of the
'Bournemouth Belle'

Kevin Robertson

www.crecy.co.uk

© Kevin Robertson 2016

ISBN 9781909328556

First published in 2016 by Crécy Publishing Ltd

Publisher's note: Every effort has been made to correctly identify and credit photographers and collections. This task is made ever more difficult where photographs have been located but upon which there is no annotation. If an error has occurred this is entirely unintentional

Printed in Slovenia by GPS Group

Noodle Books is an imprint of Crécy Publishing Limited
1a Ringway Trading Estate
Shadowmoss Road
Manchester M22 5LH

www.crecy.co.uk

Front cover No 35024 East Asiatic Company is being serviced at Boscombe shed between the down and up workings. *David Smith*

Rear cover No 35002 'Union Castle' with the up train at Eastleigh. No date is recorded but it would certainly be summer time. The presence of so many spotters is also interesting, might this have even been August and the Eastleigh Works open-day? However, putting such possibilities aside what is especially interesting is the use of the crimson and cream full-brake in place of the normal 'K' class brake at the front of the train. A late substitute perhaps and certainly the only time we have ever seen such a colour combination.

CONTENTS

Departure time at Waterloo, 1967. Passengers queue to have their tickets checked prior to boarding the train. Most will be day-trippers, emphasising the role the train played in transporting the London populace for a day out at the coast. At the barrier a Pullman steward with gold braid on his shoulders may just be seen. *Rod Hoyle*

INTRODUCTION

FOR 29 years from 1931 through to 1967 – excluding a break between 1939 and 1946 – the all-Pullman 'Bournemouth Belle' service operated between Waterloo and Bournemouth.

The train was the first new Pullman working on the former LSWR main line since 1911, when a 'Pullman Drawing Room Car' included in the formation of an ordinary service train was superseded by the modern innovation of a restaurant car accessible to the masses via the new corridor connections available between carriages. The LSWR had in fact been operating a limited Pullman service since the late 1890s – unsuccessfully as it turned out – on the Exeter line, but with more luck on Bournemouth line trains, so much so that at its peak there were four trains each way with the 'Pullman Drawing Room Car' as part of their formation.[1]

After 1911 matters rested, the principal services between the west Hampshire resort of Bournemouth[2] and London being the 2-hour non-stop express workings. These fast trains ceased in 1914, and when peace was restored in 1918 it was still some years before what was now the Southern Railway management acceded to clamour from the residents of Bournemouth to reinstate a similar service.

Accordingly on Monday 8 July 1929 the new 'Bournemouth Limited' was introduced, intended to provide the local populace with a fast service up to town in the morning with an equally rapid return in the late afternoon. This was formed of the latest corridor stock but did not include any Pullman vehicles.

From the name it might appear that the train terminated at Bournemouth; however, instead it split, the front portion continuing to Weymouth, with a further portion detached at Wareham for Swanage. Only the rearmost portion – and incidentally also the only part to carry the roof board 'Bournemouth Limited' – terminated its journey at Bournemouth West. In later years, when the train only served Bournemouth, roof boards were affixed to all vehicles.

In the reverse (up) direction, matters were slightly more involved. The Swanage portion would leave that station, join the main line at Worgret Junction (west of Wareham) and continue independently to Bournemouth West. There it would be joined to the four coaches forming part of the London service. This (semi-)complete train would then be worked around to Bournemouth Central to await the arrival of the Weymouth vehicles, which would be attached to the rear. The whole train would then set off non-stop to Waterloo. It would certainly be interesting to learn of the shunt moves involved in achieving this at both Bournemouth West and Bournemouth Central.

[1] The first Pullman cars on the LSWR date back to the 19th century when a single Pullman was included in a West of England service from Waterloo to Exeter. It was not a success and was soon withdrawn. Undaunted, the LSWR tried again by including a vehicle in the 12.30pm Waterloo to Bournemouth service and the corresponding up working. This proved much more successful and continued for many years, so much so that by 1905 the timetable showed four trains in each direction that included a 'Pullman Drawing Room Car'. Following the introduction of corridor coaches and with access to restaurant cars now available to all, Pullman usage declined.

[2] Bournemouth was geographically 'moved' into Dorset as a result of the county boundary changes of 1 April 1974.

Contrary to the commonly held belief, the 'Bournemouth Limited' was not replaced by the 'Bournemouth Belle'. Indeed, the 'Bournemouth Limited' would continue to operate under its own branding until curtailed on 9 September 1939. Following the war its successor would be the 1951 'Royal Wessex', although, now with intermediate stops at Southampton Central and Winchester City in each direction, it was generally regarded (in the up direction at least) as one of the hardest locomotive duties on the Bournemouth line due to its weight, timing and the number of station stops.

To revert to the all-Pullman service, the 'Bournemouth Belle' train dates from 5 July 1931, and although inaugurated on a Sunday, it was intended to be a daily service. Neither was this a totally new operation, as the Southern Railway already had a successful all-Pullman service in the shape of the steam-hauled 'Southern Belle', running between London and Brighton. In addition there was the 'Golden Arrow' working and the occasional use of individual Pullman vehicles included in prestigious trains operating mainly to and from Waterloo.[3]

For the first 'Bournemouth Belle', 'King Arthur' No E780 *Sir Persant*[4] left Waterloo at 10.30am, timed to pass Southampton West at 11.59am and reach Bournemouth Central at 12.39pm. Notwithstanding that on this initial run a number of passengers were members of the press or other invited guests, there were delays en route caused (it was said) by 'National League Excursion Trains'. These signal delays occurred at Malden, Esher, Fleet, Winchester, Eastleigh, and Christchurch. Despite this, there does not appear to have been any undue adverse publicity generated by the late arrival – but we are not told the actual number of minutes late! A leisurely lunch was served on the down run, concluding while the train was stabled at Bournemouth West, after which the invited guests were received at Bournemouth by the Deputy Mayor, who took them on a tour of the town before, in true English style, 'entertaining them to afternoon tea at the new pavilion'.

[3] 3. Part of the rake of Pullman stock used for the new train had its origins on the GWR; indeed, it may well have been that the offer of these vehicles to the SR had a direct bearing on the decision of the Southern Railway to commence operations. Seven Pullman cars were delivered to the GWR in 1929, these being initially used by that company within the formation of its prestige Plymouth Ocean Liner workings. Then from 8 July 1929 came the 'Torquay Pullman Limited' from Paddington, an all-Pullman service. Patronage, however, was low, so much so that the service was permanently withdrawn at the end of September 1930 and the Pullman stock moved to store at Old Oak Common, the intention at the time being to use the vehicles the following year, probably in a reversion to their earlier role within the Plymouth workings.

Who then approached who is not reported, but matters clearly moved apace, for on 1 January 1931 the seven Pullman vehicles were worked from Old Oak to Clapham Junction to begin a new lease of life on the prestige Southern Railway services. Never again would the GWR involve itself with Pullman, preferring instead to build and operate its own 'Super Saloons', which were destined to be used in similar fashion. It would not be until BR days that true Pullman services were reintroduced on the Western Region.

It may appear strange that, notwithstanding the failure of Paddington in operating Pullmans, its neighbour at Waterloo should consider introducing its own Pullman service. Here, though, we should consider the success the Southern Railway had already enjoyed with its steam-hauled 'Southern Belle' service from Victoria to Brighton (replaced by the electric 'Brighton Belle' in 1933). Paddington might therefore have ceased Pullman operation, but Waterloo would most certainly expand it. It should also be mentioned that the Southern Railway had commenced the use of Pullman vehicles within the formation of its own Ocean Liner services from and to Waterloo from 1 January 1931. Within two months passenger loadings were being reported, with 50%, or 997, of the 1,932 passengers who had used the special Ocean Liner workings in the first month of operation electing to travel Pullman and in so doing paying the additional supplement. According to the *Southern Railway Magazine* this was for services between 'Southampton and Waterloo'. It is not clear if this should be taken literally or whether it actual covered both the up and down workings. It appears that all the vehicles being used at this time were First Class only: *Ursula, Loraine, Ione, Joan, Philomel, Penelope, Adrian, Lucille, Juana, Eunice, Princess Elizabeth* and *Zena*. None of these Pullman vehicles would form part of the inaugural 'Bournemouth Belle'.

[4] The use of a 'King Arthur' engine was a late substitute for the intended member of the 'Lord Nelson' Class. Subsequently 'Lord Nelsons' would be the dominant motive power until the service was curtailed in 1939.

On the inaugural service, the return train left Bournemouth at 5.10pm and, after a permanent way slowing at Redbridge and a brief stop-over at Southampton, was due at Waterloo at 7.18pm. At least one tongue–in-cheek comment was made concerning this slowing: '…perhaps the Southern Railway was keen to allow passengers a deliberate opportunity to view work on the docks extension'! Beyond Southampton there were adverse signals at St Denys, with the service brought to a stand just south of Eastleigh. Here a recalcitrant slow train could be sidelined, after which some fast running east of Worting Junction, with a maximum of 80mph at Byfleet, helped make up the delay, culminating in an arrival at Waterloo 1 minute early.[5]

Despite being given the name 'Bournemouth Belle', half the weekday train (five cars) continued further west from Bournemouth to serve Poole, Wareham, Dorchester and Weymouth, with a corresponding service in the reverse direction. Travel to or from Weymouth added just over an hour to the journey.

Ten cars, four of which included kitchens, made up the first train, the tare weight of which was initially set at 374 tons. Accommodation was for 74 First Class and 240 Third Class passengers.

Interestingly, according to the *Railway Gazette* the timings for the new service were 2hr 9min down and 2hr 8min up. The same journal commented about how the railway might consider an alternative timing leaving Bournemouth in the late morning and calling at Southampton and Winchester, with a return around 6.00pm in the early evening. This, according to the 'RG', would give patrons 'a long afternoon in London'.[6] As it was, the initial service was indeed non-stop between Waterloo and Bournemouth, but it was quickly realised that the traffic potential for Southampton was too great an opportunity to miss, so the Southampton stop became a permanent addition to the schedule in both directions.

There are contradictory accounts of the frequency of the train as first introduced, both with regard to the number of days per week and the months of operation. This confusion appears to have continued until the start of 1936, after which we may be certain that it was a daily working. Even so, the timings varied, reportedly due to difficulties in finding a suitable path, somewhat puzzling perhaps considering that the service was regarded as a prestige working. Here, though, we may hark back to the first run with its delays in both directions – line capacity and available paths were clearly an issue for the operators even then. The schedule would eventually culminate in a pre-war arrival at Waterloo as late as 8.30pm, although in terms of pure publicity this was reported as an advantage by allowing the day-tripper more time at the coast. One early casualty was the working west beyond Bournemouth, for as early as the end of the 1931 Summer timetable low patronage meant it was withdrawn – no doubt to the accompaniment of some wry smiles at Paddington. Until July 1967 the public timetable still showed connections to and from Weymouth off the 'Belle', but invariably these involved a change of trains at Bournemouth Central.

In similar fashion the loading also varied according to the season and the day of the week. Consequently before the war there was a minimum of six and a maximum of 12 cars in use, but it was always an 'all-Pullman' train. One detail not answered is whether it was ever necessary to run a 'relief' Pullman.

With the outbreak of hostilities, the 'Bournemouth Belle' service was immediately suspended from 10 September 1939. It was reinstated on 7 October 1946 with a ten-car train hauled by 'Merchant Navy' Class engine No 21C18 *British India Line*; this and the smaller Bulleid 'Light Pacifics' would dominate the motive power on the working for the next 20 years. The timing was now

---

[5] Note that the down train was allowed a longer schedule than the corresponding up working. Possibly this was to allow for the serving of lunch at a more leisurely pace.

[6] So far as is known there was never a regular Pullman service including Winchester as a stop during Southern Railway days, while the suggestion of the *Railway Gazette* was more attuned to the 'Bournemouth Limited'. The late Derek Winkworth, in his volume *Southern Titled Trains* (David & Charles, 1988), refers to the 'Bournemouth Limited' as intended for the residents of Bournemouth to visit London and the 'Bournemouth Belle' for the residents of London to visit Bournemouth! This would certainly equate to the timings as set by the railway company.

a departure from Waterloo at 12.30 pm, calling at Southampton Central (as the former 'West' station had now been renamed) between 1.57 and 1.59pm, Bournemouth Central between 2.35 and 2.37pm, and finally Bournemouth West at 2.46pm. As might be expected, there was no reinstatement of the extension to Weymouth.

In the return direction, the train left Bournemouth West at 7.15pm, called at Bournemouth Central between 7.23 and 7.25pm, Southampton Central between 7.58 and 8.00pm, and Waterloo at 9.25pm.

The reinstated service was extremely well patronised from the outset, and one of the reasons was considered to be the ability in 1946 to forget much in the way of rationing, although this came at the price of the Pullman Supplement; however, at 3 shillings this was considered by many to be a small price to pay for such a luxury. Meals were also extra.

At the end of the 1946/47 Winter timetable, the train was accelerated to a 2-hour schedule, but at the expense of a much earlier return working, now departing from Bournemouth at 4.45pm, allowing just 2 hours there. Not surprisingly, such a move was accompanied by a chorus of protest from casual day-trippers. The 12.30pm departure for the down train, however, remained consistent.

The 2-hour timing was to be short-lived, for 5 minutes was added in 1948, while it would be a further 15 years before the same 2-hour schedule was reinstated – as late as 1963. This again would be a short-lived improvement in speed, for in 1965 the timings were again lengthened in connection with regular engineering work for the pending Bournemouth electrification. The route was also shortened slightly from 6 September 1965, following the closure of Bournemouth West station, while the 'Bournemouth Belle' itself would cease to exist after 9 July 1967, a casualty of electrification and the changing face of rail travel.

One final sop worth mentioning is that after 6 September 1965 the train both terminated at and commenced from Bournemouth Central, although the timetable still advertised the 'West' station as the final destination. A bus was therefore provided for any passengers wishing to continue to Bournemouth West, although we may be certain it was not in 'umber and cream' livery!

ACKNOWLEDGEMENTS

THE preparation of this book would not have been possible without the valued assistance of several individuals, principally (in alphabetical order): Terry Bye, Christopher Fifield, Jeffery Grayer, Roger Holmes, Tony Molyneaux, Mike Morant, Ian Shawyer, and Roger Thornton.

A number of published works, both in hard copy and electronic format, were also consulted:

Bird, John *Southern Steam Surrender* (Runpast Publishing)

Ford, Antony *Pullman Profile No 1 and No 2* (Noodle Books)

Winkworth, D. W *Southern Titled Trains* (David & Charles)

The Railway Magazine – various issues

The Railway Observer – various issues

The Railway Gazette – various issues

Southern Railway Magazine – various issues

Public and Working Timetables – various issues

Locomotive and Carriage Working Notices – various issues

SR Weekly Special Traffic Notices

Websites:

'Southern Named Trains'

'Southern E-Mail Group'

'Kent Rail'

'Coupe News'

THE ALL-PULLMAN TRAIN

No E780 *Sir Persant* heads the inaugural down train departing from Waterloo on 5 July 1931. The engine was a last-minute replacement for the booked 'Lord Nelson' and explains why it is externally far from clean. The first train consisted of Car No 40 (Third Class Brake Parlour Car), Car No 84 (Third Class Parlour Car), Car No 82 (Third Class Parlour Car), Car No 60 (Third Class Parlour Car), *Flora* (First Class Brake Parlour Car), *Montana* (First Class Brake Parlour Car), *Aurelia* (First Class Kitchen Car), Car No 81 (Third Class Kitchen Car), Car No 83 (Third Class Parlour Car), and Car No 41 (Third Class Brake Parlour Car). Among the specially invited guests on the inaugural service was Mr P. Boyle; he was Deputy Mayor of Weymouth, but his 'day job' was Traffic & Marine Manager for the GWR at Weymouth! *Southern Railway Magazine*

From the contemporary *Southern Railway Magazine*, the inaugural down train passes through the New Forest. Note the Brake Cars as the fifth and sixth vehicles; it was between these cars that the front portion would split to continue to Weymouth.

From the same source, the first service passes Christchurch.

This is the only view that could be located of the service west of Bournemouth, again on the inaugural day but this time featuring the up working (4.00pm ex-Weymouth) – presumably with No E780 again. The location is near Wishing Well Halt.

More usual motive power in the form of 'Lord Nelson' No 857 *Lord Howe* awaits departure from Waterloo some time in 1934. The formation of the train has changed already, with no Brake vehicle immediately behind the engine.

This final pre-war view shows No 862 *Lord Collingwood*. Note that again there is no headboard – when was this provided? The headcode, too, has altered, from the 'triangle' seen in the two other pre-war images to what is now the more conventional 'one up and one down' Bournemouth line route code.

At Waterloo on 7 October 1946, this is the first trip of the reinstated 'Bournemouth Belle', with No 21C18 *British India Line* quietly awaiting departure. It was a cardinal sin to allow an engine to blow off steam at the terminus, especially on this occasion with the 'top brass' present. Talking and leaning on his walking stick is Sir Eustace Missenden, General Manager, while hovering discreetly in the background in the top hat is the Waterloo station master.

Seen from the opposite platform, both engine and train are positively gleaming for the occasion – this view was taken just before the previous one, as the engine still has a tail lamp visible and the route discs are yet to be added. This is also the first time we see a headboard, albeit of rather bland design – was one used before the war? The headboard's shape would alter over the years, as can be seen from the various images that follow. For the reinstated service, ten cars were used: Car No 95 (Third Class Brake Parlour Car), Car No 60 (Third Class Kitchen Car), Car No 32 (Third Class Kitchen Car), Car No 35 (Third Class Parlour Car), *Philomel* (First Class Kitchen Car), *Lydia* (First Class Kitchen Car), *Rosemary* (First Class Parlour Car), Car No 31 (Third Class Kitchen Car), and Car No 94 (Third Class Brake Parlour Car). Only one of these, Car No 60, had featured in the first train back in 1931.

Here is a similar class of engine, but definitely on a different day – notice also that the shape of the headboard has changed. Unlike the later 'Devon Belle' train, the 'Bournemouth Belle' engine was never provided with names or wings on the smoke deflectors.

No 21C4 *Cunard White Star* passes Vauxhall at the head of ten cars soon after the reintroduction of the service. *Rev A. C. Cawston*

Preparing the Stock

UNTIL February 1960 stock for the 'Belle' was stabled at Stewarts Lane, which also dealt with the Pullman cars for the 'Golden Arrow' working. Thereafter the stabling for both trains was moved to Clapham Junction, with new arrangements made to resupply the catering and other needs at Waterloo. If necessary, restocking would also take place at Bournemouth West, or later at Bournemouth Central.

Any available locomotive type employed in carriage shunting might be used to pull the carriages for the 'Belle' from the stabling point to Waterloo, and likewise when returning empty. Here an 'M7' has the unenviable task of taking as many as 12 cars to Waterloo, including Car No 94 and *Arsonia*.

On 3 August 1964 Cars Nos 63, 62 and *Octavia* were recorded in the carriage sidings at Waterloo awaiting duty. *J. H. Meredith*

The train has arrived at Waterloo and awaits collection for Clapham. Unlike some named trains, it is believed that no name was ever carried on the corridor blank of the last vehicle.

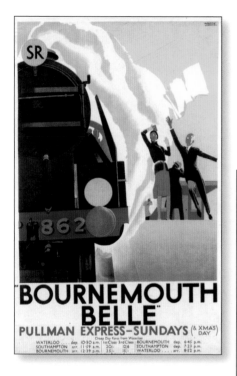

An unidentified Class 4 tank has been given the task of hauling the empty stock from the 'Belle' back to Clapham Junction.

Waterloo to Woking

In its rebuilt form, No 35018 *British India Line* awaits departure from Waterloo in 1956. This view was taken during the short time that the tender carried the first BR emblem, soon to be replaced. *F. Spencer Yates*

This time No 35025 *Brocklebank Line* is the train engine – the picture is not dated, but for the present at least the headboard is still there. It would be missing from the majority of trains in later years and as far as is known was never carried in the last days when the service was diesel-hauled.
Ian Shawyer collection

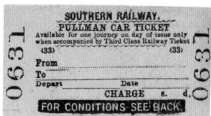

SOUTHERN RAILWAY.
PULLMAN CAR TICKET
Available for one journey on day of issue only
when accompanied by Third Class Railway Ticket
(33)   (33)
From
To
Depart _____ Date
CHARGE   s.   d.
FOR CONDITIONS SEE BACK.

No 35021 *New Zealand Line* prepares for departure. The engine may well be positioned where it is due to the length of the train, in which case a verbal authorisation to proceed was given from the platform – after authorisation by the signalman – as the train is foul of the advance track circuit. From the Southern Region Carriage Working Notice for 9 September 1963: 'Stock departure from Clapham Junction at 11.41 arrive Waterloo Platform 14 at 12.30. Load 10 cars (FX) 12 (FO).' *Ian Shawyer collection*

The curved platforms at Vauxhall are seemingly devoid of passengers as No 35014 *Nederland Line* rushes through with the down service. Note the exhaust steam hanging around the area ahead of the chimney; this was a common feature of the rebuilt engines and could almost give the impression that it was emerging from the top of the smokebox ring. *Ian Shawyer collection*

Despite the prohibition of blowing off steam and creating black smoke at Waterloo, the fireman of No 35025 *Brocklebank Line* is clearly taking the opportunity to 'put some on' as the down train reaches Vauxhall. While the car exteriors (Pullman vehicles were always 'cars' never 'coaches') are seemingly clean (and we can be sure that the interiors were), it is a pity that so many images of the train include a dirty and work-stained locomotive. Apart from a brief period when, due to staff shortages, Bournemouth shed took over supplying the engine for the 'Belle', Nine Elms depot had sole responsibility for allocating a suitable steam engine. The duty roster showed it as an '8P' working, meaning a 'Merchant Navy' would be in charge; contrary to a year or two earlier when a 'Britannia' was only a 7P. Of course this was not always the case if the allocated engine was not available for any number of reasons such as mechanical difficulty, late arrival from a previous duty, etc. Unfortunately what was generally consistent was the external appearance of the engine, cleaners being in distinctly short supply at the south London steam shed. *Norman Simmons*

For a time in 1951 one of the Southern Region-allocated 'Britannia' locomotives was allocated to the service. Here No 70009 *Alfred the Great* approaches Clapham Junction with the down train comprising at least ten cars.

From the vantage point of a conveniently located overline signal gantry, No 35027 *Port Line* is seen approaching Clapham Junction with the down train some time in 1961. As if to contradict the comments made regarding a previous image, at least it is possible to determine that this is a green-painted engine! It is likely that every member of the 30-strong 'Merchant Navy' Class worked the train at some time, together with a goodly proportion of the 'Light Pacifics'. *Meteor Film Services*

A regular performer on main-line duties until the end of steam was No 35008 *Orient Line*, seen here just after passing Wimbledon. The picture is undated and there is unfortunately no obvious train identification, although the full set of Pullmans leaves no doubt that this is the 'Belle'.

A 'Light Pacific' in the form of No 34001 is in charge of the down service on 19 April 1966. The location is the same as that seen in the previous view, Wimbledon. Note the smokebox ash that has not been swept off the framing. The engine is AWS-fitted, having the battery box located on the front framing immediately above the buffer beam. This engine had formerly carried the name *Exeter*. *Norman Simmons*

No 35016 *Elders Fyffes* crosses from the main to the relief line at Raynes Park with the down train. This was certainly not a normal event and likely to be a prelude to a diversion due to engineering work or another obstruction.

There is heat haze and just a wisp of smoke from the chimney as another grubby 'rebuilt' 'Merchant Navy' approaches Surbiton. At the rear of the train it is just possible to identify a blue/grey Full Brake. *Peter Knottley*

Below: The date is slightly earlier as No 35014 *Nederland Line* passes on the down through line at Surbiton. The engine still retains its yellow stripes, while again it will also be noted that the first vehicle is not a Brake. *Arthur Taylor*

No 34044 *Woolacombe* approaches Walton-on-Thames in 1967, the steam train seeming as dated as the cars in the road below – a Vauxhall Cresta, Austin A30, Mk 1 Ford Cortina and a Ford Anglia (not that we remember any, of course...!). *Rod Hoyle*

As a late substitution for a failed 'Pacific' or diesel, Nine Elms has turned out 'Standard 5' No 73043, seen passing Weybridge with the down working on an unknown date, but probably 1967. By the end of 1966 the last 'K' Class Brake coaches had been withdrawn from use, their place taken by Mark 1 Brake Vans (BGs); the saga involving their liveries is discussed later. *Keith Lawrence*

Here is another 'Merchant Navy' substitution, but two years earlier on 9 March 1965. This time it is No 34060 *25 Squadron*, also clearly with steam on as it passes through Weybridge with a proper rake of cars in tow. *P. J. Lynch*

An unidentified 'Merchant Navy' passes Byfleet Junction near Woking with the down train in Southern days. As with the other images from that time, the majority of cars seen are of the 12-wheel type, which meant that the train weight might approach 500 tons.

A begrimed No 34025 *Whimple* approaches Woking with the down train. Assuming that the service is running to time (and the down working was reasonably reliable), it should just be approaching 1.00pm – 30 minutes after departure from Waterloo. *Martin Upward*

Passing a variety of platform clutter associated with the steam railway, a 'Squadron' 'Light Pacific' is seen on the through road at Woking, again with the down train. Clearly 1.00pm was not the busiest period on the platforms! *Peter Knottley*

WOKING TO NORTHAM JUNCTION

Watched by an enthusiastic group, No 35017 *Belgian Marine*, in its rebuilt state, heads the down train at Pirbright Junction. This was the location for the divergence of the line to Farnham, Alton and the mid-Hants route to Winchester. Until electrification of the Bournemouth line, the third rail was only on the slow lines but, as can be seen in this view from 10 September 1966, the through lines have also been so fitted. *Roger Thornton*

It is May 1965 and the down train is passing a group of men working on the newly laid concrete troughing that will be used to hold signalling and telephone cables in connection with the pending installation of MAS. The engine's identity is not confirmed but it is definitely a 'Merchant Navy' and this time with a distinct underlying hint of green livery. The location is the eastern approach to Farnborough where, for the time being, it is still only the slow lines that have the third rail.

What is probably a 1951 image shows No 70009 *Alfred the Great* with the down train on the curve through Farnborough station – in recent times referred to as 'Farnborough Main'. It is strange to think that at this time the Southern Region possessed no fewer than 143 'Pacific'-type engines, including three members of the 'Britannia' Class. The magnificent signal gantry, sometimes referred to as a 'signal bridge', has a number of low-pressure pneumatic signals, which served the railway well until replaced by colour lights. *E. C. Griffiths*

A splendid sight in full Southern Railway livery (but sporting its newly acquired British Railways cabside number), No 35017, formerly 21C17 *Belgian Marine*, speeds past Bramshott Halt west of Farnborough. The train appears to consist primarily of 12-wheel cars complete with 'Bournemouth Belle' roofboards. *R. F. Dearden*

Opposite: In this view, taken on the racing stretch of the main line, a Southern-liveried 'Merchant Navy' with a 10-car working shows evidence that the fireman has recently been adding a few shovelfuls to the fire. In the early 1950s the timings for the down train as far as Southampton were: Waterloo 12.30pm, Clapham Junction (pass) 12.37pm, Woking (pass) 1.00pm, Worting Junction (pass) 1.26pm, Winchester Junction (pass) 1.41½pm, Eastleigh (pass) 1.50pm, St Denys (pass) 1.58pm, and Southampton Central (arr) 2.03pm. *R. F. Dearden*

Ten cars plus a blue BG make up the formation this time, with a grimy 'Light Pacific' in charge. The location is the deep cutting near Winchfield.

Heading ever further west, we see No 35012 *United States Lines* near Hook. Compared with several of the images seen earlier, this was the second style of headboard carried. *M. W. Earley*

THE ALL PULLMAN

BOURNEMOUTH *BELLE*

DAILY THROUGHOUT THE YEAR

Also near to Hook and passing another of the pneumatic signalling gantries, No 35019 *French Line CGT* is on the down working on 20 April 1962. The Southern Railway had operated three all-Pullman services with the suffix 'Belle': the 'Brighton Belle' (originally the 'Southern Belle'), the 'Devon Belle', introduced in the last year of the independent Southern Railway in 1947, and the 'Bournemouth Belle', seen here. Additionally in 1948 the newly formed British Railways would bring in the 'Thanet Belle', later renamed the 'Kentish Belle'. *Tony Molyneaux*

THE ALL PULLMAN

BOURNEMOUTH BELLE

DAILY THROUGHOUT THE YEAR

THE
BRIGHTON
BELLE

THE
BOURNEMOUTH
BELLE

SERVICES & FARES

until 4 September 1966

Steaming well and probably travelling in excess of 70mph, No 34001 (formerly *Exeter*) heads the 'Belle' probably in the period 1965/66. Note the lack of any nameplates, while on the track itself there is clear evidence of relaying and the provision of the third rail.

Belgian Marine was obviously a popular choice of loco for the train, seen here again passing through Platform 3 at Basingstoke with the first style of headboard. Although previously reproduced elsewhere, this image is included for its rarity factor – how many colour views exist of the train in 1947/48? On the extreme right is the bay platform, No 1, once used for trains to Alton, while on the extreme opposite side is the Great Western station used by services to Reading. *Colour-Rail*

The famed location of Worting Junction, west of Basingstoke, was the point of divergence (convergence if travelling in the opposite direction) of the West of England and Bournemouth lines. No 35010 *Blue Star* is seen using the newly installed (1957) high-speed turnout from the down through West of England route to the Bournemouth line, the speed limit for which had recently been raised to 70mph. As well as facing crossovers between all the through and local lines at this point, there was also an emergency trailing crossover seen in the background. Worting was the westernmost limit of the four-track section from Waterloo. *British Railways*

On 4 May 1951 No 70009 has taken the Bournemouth line and is heading towards Southampton. In the background is Battledown flyover (to give it its proper name – it was rarely referred to as 'Worting flyover') where the up Bournemouth line was carried over the West of England route. *E. D. Bruton*

At the same point on 19 August 1958 No 35020 *Bibby Line* is on the down working while passing in the opposite direction, climbing the 1 in 106 gradient leading to the flyover, is probably the 11.16am Bournemouth to Newcastle through service. *Roger Thornton*

Because of its late afternoon running time (about 4.45pm from Bournemouth Central), photographs of the up service are less common than the down and of course restricted to certain times of the year. Here, however, 'Merchant Navy' No 35011 *General Steam Navigation* is photographed on the approach to Micheldever, close to the summit of the long 22-mile 1 in 250 climb from Eastleigh and therefore likely to be travelling at 50-60mph at this point. *F. R. Hebron*

From a similar angle and again at Micheldever, what could well be No 35028 *Clan Line* heads the 12-car Friday train. Loadings would vary but after the war there were typically 12 cars on Friday, with 11 cars on other days for the duration of the summer timetable. For winter, the loading was nine cars on Monday and Saturday, ten on Tuesday, Wednesday and Thursday, and 11 on Sunday. Micheldever once had a large number of sidings for both local goods as well as stock storage and oil distribution. Already in this view many are out of use, and the layout was later rationalised so that since 1967 it has consisted of just up and down lines with no passing loops.

This time we know for certain it is No 35028 *Clan Line*, having left Waller's Ash Tunnel and shortly to pass Winchester Junction signal box. The industrial-type buildings on the left are part of an egg-producing facility. *Tony Molyneaux*

Until the early 1960s it was possible to obtain a lineside/photographic permit, thus legally allowed to 'trespass' – albeit subject to certain restrictions. Having such a facility gave one the opportunity to capture some different angles in photography, such as here, with No 35012 *United States Lines* on the down train between Winchester Junction and Winchester City station. *Henry Meyer*

It's the evening of 3 May 1963 and a busy time at Winchester City. No 35011 *General Steam Navigation* is on the up 'Belle' while in the yard 'S15' No 30498 waits to follow with an up freight. *M. J. Fox*

Seen from the opposite side of the line from the up yard at Winchester City, No 35016 *Elders Fyffes* approaches with the down train. *R. S. Knight*

This interesting view shows the train in the down platform at Winchester City, the engine being another 'Merchant Navy', No 35018 *British India Line*, prior to rebuilding. It looks as if the train is stationary – note the steam from the cylinder cock – and also what is probably a railwayman on the platform. But why and, of course, when? Was it a mechanical problem, a passenger emergency, a signal stop, or perhaps even the very rare occurrence of a special stop? *R. Blencowe*

It's late evening, hence the long shadows as No 35008 *Orient Line* passes under the Upper High Street bridge at Winchester bound for Waterloo. *Ian Shawyer collection*

Lunchtime in the cutting by St James Lane just south of Winchester in January 1965. *Rod Hoyle*

Reflections at Winchester, 1966. *Rod Hoyle*

Recollections by Ian Shawyer, image by Rod Hoyle. 'Memories of the "Bournemouth Belle" will live with me for ever. Luxurious-looking chocolate and cream-coloured coaches with gold- lettered names and numbers painted on the sides, speeding through Winchester City, the rear coach rocking from side to side like a rock 'n' roll dancer as it disappeared from view; the sound of a Bulleid whistle echoing through the station cutting; one knew it was either the 1.40pm (down) or 5.40pm (up). You could set your watch by "Bournemouth Belle" time.

'Also of Stan Mitchell, long-time station announcer at Southampton Central. The arrival of the "Belle" was a time for Stan to shine. His precise informative announcements were a joy to behold. In his Hampshire drawl he would start by saying "Waterloo only", in so doing expressing the importance of the "Belle" by advising passengers where to board. I had the privilege of travelling on the train twice in the 1960s, both occasions being on the home run back to London Waterloo. Apart from the railway fare, one needed to purchase a "Pullman Supplement" to travel on this train, and of course food and drink was extra. On both my trips I boarded the "Belle" at Bournemouth Central, where immediately there was a certain excitement in setting foot on a train that usually I only ever saw rushing through Winchester City. As the "Belle" arrived, so car doors were opened by smartly attired Pullman-uniformed staff inviting you in. At the same time the attendants swung a small board outward to display the appropriate Pullman car letter. Upon boarding, you did not find your seat – you were shown to it – all ready for afternoon tea, extra of course, but it was expected that you would participate.

'That tea consisted of a hot buttered and toasted teacake, a round of triangle-cut sandwiches followed by a slice of Genoa cake plus of course lashings of tea served in a silver teapot. Afterwards there was plenty of time to sit back, relax and enjoy the rest of the journey to London Waterloo.

'"Merchant Navy" No 35021 *New Zealand Line* was the engine on that first journey, while poignantly I also travelled on the last up working on Sunday 9 July 1967, this time behind Brush Type 4 No D1924, which as No 47810 is still running around the network. For that last run I was in Car No 76, which also still survives and now does service on the Bluebell Railway carrying the name *Lillian*.'

With evening shadows starting to lengthen, No 34097 *Holsworthy* appears to be working well as the up train approaches St Cross, just south of Winchester, in May 1965. *Rod Hoyle*

A location now changed beyond recognition, this is Shawford Junction where the old brick overbridge has long been replaced by a massive concrete structure carrying the M3 motorway over the railway. Years earlier, No 35017 *Belgian Marine* in green but with black skirts passes with the down working on 6 October 1953. *R. Blencowe*

VENICE SIMPLON-ORIENT-EXPRESS

Passing a goods yard seemingly devoid of any meaningful traffic, No 35012 *United States Lines* is on the up train at Shawford on 19 July 1959. Officially the yard here was still in use, although it would finally close in July of the following year. *Tony Molyneaux*

Two trains, but travelling in opposite directions. The down 'Belle' is seen passing a pull-push Southampton-Alton local at Otterbourne, south of Shawford. *Henry Meyer*

This time the train is recorded north of Eastleigh with tank cars (just like Pullman vehicles, tank wagons were also referred to as 'cars') for Fawley in the East yard. The engine is No 35016 *Elders Fyffes*. *Ian Shawyer collection*

Shattering the lunchtime peace at Eastleigh, No 35022 *Holland-America Line* is caught passing beneath Bishopstoke Road bridge at Eastleigh in about 1960. *I. D. Hodson*

Another evening image, and this time No 35014 *Nederland Line* is on the up through line at Eastleigh on 11 September 1965. The first vehicle is unusual and certainly not regularly seen. An image we were shown but were unable to obtain for this book was of the train with a Bullion Van as the first vehicle. Whether this was purloined at the last minute due to the non-availability of a BG was not reported. At the end of what were then Platforms 1 and 2, the rectangular board warned of the dire consequences locomen faced if they failed to take the official walking route from the station to the shed. *Ian Shawyer collection*

A more common first vehicle – certainly in later years – is seen here at the head of the down train at Eastleigh in 1963, behind No 35007 *Aberdeen Commonwealth*, seemingly with a few steam leaks that should not be present. *Ian Shawyer collection*

A grimy No 34004 *Yeovil* passes an equally grimy 'Hampshire' diesel unit with the down train on 7 May 1966. The rear of the train is just passing the end of the platforms at Eastleigh, and it will reach Southampton Central within the next 13 minutes. *Tony Molyneaux*

'Merchant Navy' No 35024 *East Asiatic Company* is seen here for the first time on the service. The location is just south of Eastleigh with the wartime Stoneham sidings on the left; these were provided during the Second World War to stable locomotives away from the main steam shed, thus reducing the risk of widespread damage from enemy action. The photographer, the late Les Elsey, was active in the area for many years, employed as a fitter at the nearby diesel depot. It was thus a small step to walk across from the steam shed – out of camera on the right – to record the afternoon working. Note the edge of a railwayman's allotment on the right. *Les Elsey*

At the south end of Stoneham sidings and its controlling signal box – where there was also an occupation crossing – 'Britannia' No 70009 is seen again with the up train. On the left-hand side of the line is the expanse of today's Southampton (Eastleigh) Airport. *P. Ransome Wallis*

The same engine is seen again at the rarely recorded location of Northam Junction. In June 1951 the up train is just negotiating the sharp curve at Northam before commencing the run on basically straight track for the next 25 miles as far as Worting Junction, albeit much of it on a rising gradient.

THE BOURNEMOUTH BELLE

" I travel for travel's sake. The great affair is to move," said a writer of renown. But that was in a more leisured world, methinks. To-day, alas, not many of us have time to travel for travel's sake, but most of us have to move. And when we move we need both speed and comfort. These are ours if we travel by the BELLES, the all-Pullman luxury trains of the Southern Region.

The BOURNEMOUTH BELLE runs daily in both directions throughout the year, stopping only at Southampton. She provides a smooth, comfortable journey, excellent meals *en route*, and courteous attention.

As on the other BELLES the number of passengers is limited to the number of seats, and seats are reserved in advance by applying to the Station Master's Office at Waterloo, Southampton or Bournemouth.

And if in the Bournemouth area during the summer months it is worth remembering that Holiday Run-About Tickets provide unlimited rail travel for 7 days for the modest price of 12s. 6d. There are 4 varieties from which to choose (Areas 8, 9, 10 and 11) and leaflets giving details and map can be had free of charge at Southern Region stations.

BRITISH RAILWAYS

DAILY SERVICE

12.30 p.m. dep.	WATERLOO	arr. 6.50 p.m.
1.58 p.m. arr.	SOUTHAMPTON CENTRAL	dep. 5.20 p.m.
2.40 p.m. arr.	BOURNEMOUTH CENTRAL	dep. 4.45 p.m.
2.52 p.m. arr.	BOURNEMOUTH WEST	dep. 4.34 p.m.

PULLMAN CAR SUPPLEMENTARY FEE

	1st Cl.	3rd Cl.
WATERLOO—SOUTHAMPTON	3/6	2/-
WATERLOO—BOURNEMOUTH	5/-	3/-
BOURNEMOUTH—SOUTHAMPTON	2/-	1/6

For details of " Brighton Belle," " Devon Belle " and " Thanet Belle " please ask for separate folders.

AD.6005   10,000   1/9/49   Printed in Great Britain by McCorquodale & Co. Ltd., Ldn.—52618

This fabulous image shows No 34064 *Fighter Command* having come off the curve at Northam and now passing Tunnel Junction on the last leg of the run to Southampton Central. *Henry Meyer*

SOUTHAMPTON TO BOURNEMOUTH

The now preserved and popular No 35028 *Clan Line* arrives at Platform 1 at Southampton Central with the down train on 6 February 1960. *Tony Molyneaux*

Possibly the first post-war run again, on 7 October 1946, this time the train is seen departing from Southampton Central; certainly it is the same engine, No 21C18 *British India Line*. The signals are off for the main line, thus avoiding the island platforms at Millbrook. The train's departure is also being watched from the signal box.

Twelve-wheel Car No 96 (complete with roof board) at Southampton Central.

This time it is a clean engine, No 35007 *Aberdeen Commonwealth*, at the same location. For many years it was the practice to keep a stand-by engine in the bay at Southampton Central in the event of difficulties with the down working. That was of no use on one occasion when an engine failure occurred at Basingstoke and a rather decrepit 'U' Class was hastily summoned to take what was by now the late-running service to Southampton. Fortunately, by the time Southampton was reached Eastleigh had managed to summon a more suitable replacement. Assuming all was well, the stand-by engine would follow later with a Bournemouth stopping service. Possibly this practice ceased after an alteration to the timetable; perhaps surprisingly, there was no similar arrangement for up trains.

Here's No 70009 again, with nameplates clearly visible. On this day, Saturday 6 October 1951, the stand-by engine was a 'Lord Nelson', which also acted as station pilot.

No 35017 *Belgian Marine* takes water at Southampton Central on 19 February 1964 – water would be taken here by both the down and up trains. At the time when Nine Elms men and a Nine Elms-based engine were responsible for the working, the crew would book on at 11.20am to an already prepared engine. They would leave the depot at 11.35am (12.01pm on Saturdays) and reverse back to Waterloo, where the Pullman cars would already be waiting; arrival at Waterloo on Monday-Friday was 11.53am, Saturday 12.15pm. After working the train to Bournemouth West, and with the engine released, they would reverse to Branksome depot for servicing. No set time was given for arrival at or departure from Branksome, although the engine and crew would be ready to depart from Bournemouth West at 4.34pm, arriving back at Waterloo at 6.50pm. There the men would be relieved and a replacement crew would take the engine to the shed for disposal. *Ian Shawyer collection*

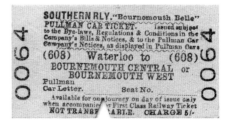

In Southern days again, this time there are two engines alongside, the 'T9' due to follow later with the Bournemouth stopping service. Whether it would have been much use had the 'Merchant Navy' needed substituting is debatable. *Ian Shawyer collection*

Without any obvious trace of a slip, rebuilt 'Merchant Navy' No 35022 *Holland-America Line* gets away from Southampton Central with the down train.

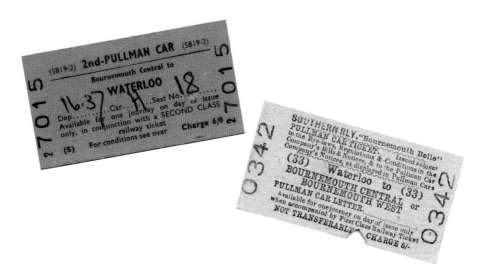

During the time when the 'Merchant Navy' Class was temporarily withdrawn due to axle fatigue, several 'V2s' were loaned from the Eastern Region for the prestige services. Here No 60893, temporarily based at Nine Elms, is seen leaving Southampton, next stop Bournemouth! (Engine types known to have been used on the train from its inception were 'King Arthurs', 'Lord Nelsons', Merchant Navies', 'West Country'/'Battle of Britain' 'Light Pacifics', 'V2s', 'Britannias' and Standard Class 5s, followed by diesel locos Nos 10000/10001, 10201/10202, D65xx and Brush Type 4 types.)

It's grimy engine time again, as No 34104 *Bere Alston* blasts its way west on 19 March 1966. *Tony Molyneaux*

An equally grimy No 35019 *French Line CGT* is seen near the same spot on 14 April 1964. Note that the first vehicle is a Second Class Parlour Car, rather than the more usual Brake. *Tony Molyneaux*

On 5 March 1967, with just four months of service left before both train and engine would pass into history, No 35007, formerly named *Aberdeen Commonwealth*, has steam to spare as it heads west from Southampton towards Millbrook. The first vehicle is a green Mk 1 BG (Full Brake), which has replaced the more usual 'K' Class Pullman Brake Car. The story of how the BGs came to be used on the 'Belle' is an interesting one. Logic dictated that in order to maintain the semblance of an all-Pullman service, something was needed to replace the Brake Cars, but not an ordinary passenger-carrying vehicle – hence the use of the BG. However, at the time those available to the Southern were invariably either maroon or green, the latter being repainted maroon vehicles. Then one day the Yard Master at Clapham Junction – where the Pullman stock for the 'Belle' was now stabled – happened to notice a chocolate and cream-liveried BG in an inter-regional stock transfer train and thought it was just the thing for the Pullman. Acting on his own initiative, he quickly substituted in the stock train another van that happened to be on hand. The Western Region was not best pleased by the Southern's action, as this was still the period when chocolate and cream stock was specifically allocated to the WR's named trains. Nonetheless, the purloined BG and another in the same livery were used for the 'Belle', although on occasions maroon, green and later blue/grey examples were also recorded. There is even photographic evidence of a maroon and cream BG being used, although it is thought that this was a rare occasion in earlier years when a 'K' Class Brake was temporarily unavailable.

No 35029 *Ellerman Lines* – now 'sectioned' in the National Railway Museum – shows the difference between a clean and well-looked-after engine and the grime more associated with the later days. Again the engine has steam to spare.

Opposite: On 31 May 1963, with the towers of Southampton power station in the background, No 35005 *Canadian Pacific* heads a 12-coach down service, the weight of which is probably in the order of 500 tons.

The first station out of Southampton is Millbrook, where the fast lines bypass the island platform on either side. The two lines on the extreme right are the entry to and exit from the Western Docks. No 35012 *United States Lines* and a maroon BG head up the train. *R. A. Panting*

No 35014 *Nederland Line* passes the point where the dock lines peel off. On the left can just be seen a small part of Millbrook goods yard, latterly a Freightliner terminal. *Ian Shawyer collection*

A grimy 'Battle of Britain' 'Pacific' passes the sidings at Redbridge with the down train. *Roger Holmes*

Also at Redbridge is another 'Light Pacific', but this time one that can be identified by its name – No 34040 *Crewkerne*. *Roger Holmes*

What a difference the sun makes! Here we have the combination of a Pullman Brake and a BG, but with the usual filthy engine. The location is the old bridge over the causeway at Redbridge. *Roger Holmes*

On 26 August 1951 No 35011 *General Steam Navigation* still carries the Southern green and yellow stripes but with 'British Railways' emblazoned on the tender. The load for this down service is a dozen 12-wheel cars, including one recently outshopped as witnessed by its clean roof. *Donovan Box*

Out in the New Forest, No 34101 *Hartland* is seen near Beaulieu Road station – more recently renamed 'Ashurst New Forest'. *John Davenport*

Opposite: Just to prove that No 35005 *Canadian Pacific* was clean at least once, the train is seen having just passed through Totton. The single stop signal applies to trains off the Fawley branch, being the single line of rails immediately to the right of the train. *Roger Holmes*

Leaning to the curve between Beaulieu and Brockenhurst is No 34087 *145 Squadron*. *Roger Holmes*

This is believed to be No 35027 *Port Line*, but it is hard to distinguish fully due to the dirt. *Roger Holmes*

Hitherto unrecorded in this book, No 35001 *Channel Packet* has just passed a hitherto unrecorded location, the level crossing at Brockenhurst, and is seen entering the station.

Opposite: No 34013 *Okehampton* has unofficial white embellishments, possibly as a result of recent enthusiast special duty.
Roger Holmes

On the other side of Brockenhurst was Lymington Junction, where the Lymington branch and Ringwood line diverged on opposite sides of the main line. No 34061 *73 Squadron*, possibly a late substitute for a 'Merchant Navy', is passing the controlling signal box on 29 May 1950. *J. C. Flemons*

Now comes the climb of Sway Bank. The engine is No 35014 *Nederland Line*, affording us the opportunity to record that the train nameboard was not in Pullman colours! *Les Elsey*

No 35013 *Blue Funnel* and a blue/grey BG head the down train at New Milton on 20 August 1966. *Mark B. Warburton, courtesy of Mrs Margaret Warburton*

Not far from journey's end, No 35005 negotiates the curve through Christchurch with the down working on 16 March 1964. *Mark B. Warburton, courtesy of Mrs Margaret Warburton*

Following a signal check, No 35014 crosses the River Stour near Christchurch with the down train on 13 April 1958. *Colin Boocock*

No 35015 *Rotterdam Lloyd* passes a station now long closed, Boscombe on the outskirts of Bournemouth. *Ian Shawyer collection*

Above: On a different occasion the same engine enters Bournemouth Central station with the down train. *Sharpe Photographic*

Left: The long down platform at Bournemouth Central could be used by two trains simultaneously if required, although on 19 June 1959 No 35019 *French Line CGT* has the complete length to itself. Bournemouth loco depot is on the left. *Tony Molyneaux*

On this occasion, 14 February 1960, the western end of the platform is occupied by a stopping service to Weymouth behind No 75066, due to follow *Nederland Line* once the route is clear. *Ian Shawyer collection*

This photograph provides a good view of the actual platform crossover, as No 35021 *New Zealand Line* heads the down service on 1 June 1957. *Ian Shawyer collection*

Newly repainted *Lucille* is seen on 31 March 1963. This particular car would be included in the final service on 9 July 1967.

Car No 62 at Bournemouth Central on 12 April 1963.

No 35005 takes the curve leading from Gas Works Junction on the Weymouth line towards Bournemouth West. The train is now 110 miles from its departure point and very close to its destination. *Ian Shawyer collection*

No 35027 *Port Line* leaves the terminus at Bournemouth West for Waterloo on 14 June 1965. *Derek Cross*

Upon arrival at Bournemouth West, the stock would be drawn clear and stabled ready for servicing. In view of the limited time available between the down arrival and up departure, the opportunity to do this was limited and it would not be too long before the stock for the return working was being hauled back into the platform.

In this earlier view, Class 'O2' 0-4-4T No 30212 is acting as carriage shunter, while passengers wait to join the train at Bournemouth West.

The up train has just left Bournemouth West on the first stage of its journey to Waterloo.

No 35024 *East Asiatic Company* is being serviced at Boscombe shed between the down and up workings. *David Smith*

NINE ELMS DUTY No. 33		
8 P. (Merchant Navy Class)		
(Pullman Train)		
SATURDAYS EXCEPTED		
—	Nine Elms ...	...11.35 a.m. ‖
11.53 a.m.	Waterloo ...	...12.30 p.m. P
2.52 p.m.	Bournemouth West	**‖
**	Branksome	**‖
**	Bournemouth West	4.34 p.m. P
6.50 p.m.	Waterloo	7.23 p.m. ‖
7.35 p.m.	Nine Elms ...	—
SATURDAYS ONLY		
—	Nine Elms ...	...12. 1 p.m. ‖
12.15 p.m.	Waterloo ...	...12.30 p.m. P
2.52 p.m.	Bournemouth West	**‖
**	Branksome	**‖
**	Bournemouth West	4.34 p.m. P
Up to 11th September		
6.50 p.m.	Waterloo	7.53 p.m. E
8. 3 p.m.	Clapham Jn.	**‖
**	Nine Elms	‖
18th September only		
6.50 p.m.	Waterloo	7.32 p.m. E
7.42 p.m.	Clapham Jc.	**‖
**	Nine Elms	‖

Nine Elms Men.
Off No. 94, prepare.
1st set on duty 11.20 a.m., relieved at 6.50 p.m.
S.X.—Men off No. 435, relieve and Waterloo 6.50 p.m. and work to Nine Elms and dispose.
2nd set (S.O. up to 27/6 and from 4/9) On duty 6.20 p.m., relieve 6.50 p.m., work and dispose.
S.O.—(3/7 to 28/8) Off No. 503, relieve at Waterloo 6.50 p.m., work and dispose.

DIVERSIONS

The unusual sight of a single 'D65xx' (later Class 33) on the down 'Belle'. No D6503 has just left Alton and is about to start the 1 in 60 climb of the mid-Hants line towards Medstead. The mid-Hants line was a regular diversionary route for both this and other Bournemouth line services when the main line was inaccessible between Pirbright Junction and Winchester Junction. The rails on the right – note the metal sleepers and fastenings – form the northern stub of the erstwhile Meon Valley route, then in use solely as a long siding as far as Farringdon. *Ian Shawyer collection*

Above: Guildford has turned out its solitary Standard Class 3 tender engine, No 77014, to act as pilot to No 34102 *Lapford* for the down train, seen here on the climb to Medstead on 17 September 1966. *Roger Thornton*

Right: Believed to have been photographed on 5 March 1961, this combination of No 31628 and 35030 *Elder Dempster Lines* with the diverted train was recorded near Alresford. Examples of other known diversions over the mid-Hants line around this time and involving double-heading were on 10 and 16 January 1961 when BR Class 4 tank engines Nos 80144 and 80138 respectively were used. On 18 January that year, a combination of No 34044 *Woolacombe* assisted by No 76065 was used. It is likely that the assisting engines were just used between Alton and either Alresford or Winchester. *Tony Molyneaux*

Easier going now on the mid-Hants line, as an unidentified 'D65xx' approaches Itchen Abbas. Note the combination of a 'K' Class Brake Car at the front and a blue/grey BG at the rear. On more than one occasion a diesel locomotive of this type was used to bring the empty stock of the train from the sidings at Clapham Junction to Waterloo ready for departure. However, for the regular service a single diesel locomotive of this type was found to be incapable of keeping to the schedule, so double-heading was quickly resorted to. *John Bailey*

If the main line was obstructed south of Eastleigh and/or the mid-Hants route was not available, the diversionary route was via the 'Portsmouth Direct' line from Woking to Havant, then through Cosham and Fareham and along the curved Netley line to Southampton. Such was the case on 20 March 1966 when No 34095 *Brentor* was recorded near Haslemere with the down working. An earlier diversion along the same route had seen No 34010 *Sidmouth* with the down Sunday working on 28 October 1962, while 13 March 1966 was another day the train was similarly diverted. *Roger Thornton*

A very unusual diversion for the train occurred on 1 November 1964 when, due to engineering work both near Swaythling (south of Eastleigh) and also at Peasmarsh Junction (on the 'Portsmouth Direct' line), the train was worked to Eastleigh, then Fareham, where reversal took place. Arriving at Fareham from the Eastleigh direction is No 34082 *615 Squadron*; another locomotive will come on the other end to take the train back towards Southampton via the Netley line. *John Bailey*

Opposite top: The same train awaits departure from Fareham. The cleared signal at the end of the platform is for No 34082, which will run forward on to the Gosport line as a temporary measure. *John Bailey*

Bottom: Setting off back towards Southampton, the train is now headed by a very grimy No 34046 *Braunton*. Note that, as the train has not been shunted across to the normal departure platform, this will be a hand-signalled move with the associated crossovers clipped and padlocked. *John Bailey*

Displaying the headcode for the Fareham to Southampton line, No 34010 *Sidmouth* rounds the curve at Bursledon under the watchful eye of the signalman. *Roger Holmes*

DIESEL FINALE

At the end of 1966 eight Brush Type 4 diesel locomotives were transferred from the Western Region (mainly from Cardiff Canton depot) for use on the Southern Region. The reason for this was a shortage of suitable express motive power on the Southern, so many steam engines having been withdrawn. Another factor was the increasingly run-down condition of the surviving locos, meaning that a 450-500-ton train was simply beyond their capabilities. An example of this was on 29 December 1966 when No 34077 ran short of steam twice on the down train, including the necessity for a 20-minute stop in an attempt to rectify matters, before the crew were faced with no choice but to give up. The train had to be rescued with the aid of the diesel pilot at Woking. WR-based diesels were selected as these had both steam and electric heating, whereas the first choice for the transfer, Eastern Region locomotives, were only fitted for electric train heating. The diesels were intended for use on the principal services, including the 'Bournemouth Belle', although such was their poor reliability at the time that substitutions would take place almost right to the end of the life of the train. Here No D1925 is in charge of the down working at Vauxhall.

Another Brush Type 4 (later Class 47) is seen slightly further west, in the cutting beyond Clapham Junction. Officially the train was given over to diesel haulage from 2 January 1967. *J. Grayer collection*

Sunshine in the New Forest, probably near Beaulieu Road. *Roger Holmes*

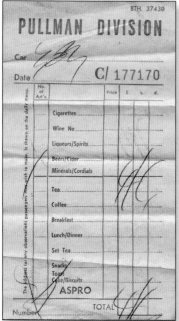

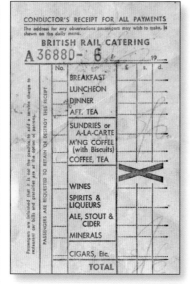

The only located image of a pair of Class 33 diesels on the train shows them passing the carriage sidings at Oatlands Cutting with the up working. *Keith Lawrence*

Almost the very last time steam had charge of the train, No 34025 *Whimple* has just passed Weybridge on the down service on Monday 3 July 1967, just six days before both steam and the 'Bournemouth Belle' would cease to exist. The final steam workings were two days later on 5 July when Nos 34024 *Tamar Valley* and 34036 *Westward Ho* had charge of the down and up workings respectively, again deputising for a failed diesel. *Keith Lawrence*

On the last day, Sunday 9 July 1967, No D1924 passes the now redundant signal box at Hook (closed from 23 October 1966) with the final down working. Every effort had been made by both the enthusiast fraternity and railwaymen in the diagram office to have a steam engine rostered for the final day, but this was not to be. *Keith Lawrence*

The same train is seen again on the causeway at Redbridge, west of Southampton. *Alistair Jeffery*

Car No 34 stands at Southampton Central on the last day – note that the distinctive Pullman table lamps have already been removed. The formation of the final workings, both up and down, was No D1924 with M80869 (BR Mk 1 Full Brake), Car No 75 (Third Class Parlour Car), Car No 61 (Third Class Kitchen Car), Car No 64 (Third Class Parlour Car), *Ursula* (First Class Parlour Car), *Phyllis* (First Class Kitchen Car), *Lucille* (First Class Parlour Car), *Aquila* (First Class Kitchen Car), Car No 76 (Third Class Parlour Car), Car No 34 (Second Class Parlour Car), and E80631 (BR Mk 1 Full Brake).

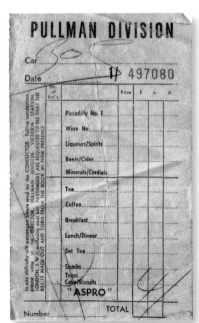

THE
"BOURNEMOUTH BELLE"

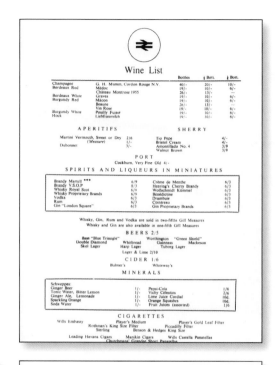

Wine List

		Bottles	½ Bott.	¼ Bott.
Champagne	G. H. Mumm, Cordon Rouge N.V.	40/-	20/-	10/-
Bordeaux Red	Médoc	19/-	10/-	6/-
	Château Montrose 1955	26/-	13/-	—
Bordeaux White	Graves	19/-	10/-	6/-
Burgundy Red	Mâcon	19/-	10/-	6/-
	Beaune	26/-	13/-	—
	Vin Rosé	19/-	10/-	6/-
Burgundy White	Pouilly Fuissé	19/-	10/-	6/-
Hock	Liebfraumilch	19/-	10/-	6/-

APERITIFS   SHERRY

Martini Vermouth, Sweet or Dry	2/6	Tio Pepe	4/-
(Measure)	1/-	Bristol Cream	4/-
Dubonnet	3/-	Amontillado No. 4	3/9
		Walnut Brown	3/9

PORT
Cockburn, Very Fine Old 4/-

SPIRITS AND LIQUEURS IN MINIATURES

Brandy Martell ***	6/9	Crème de Menthe	6/3
Brandy V.S.O.P	8/3	Heering's Cherry Brandy	6/3
Whisky Royal Scot	6/9	Wolfschmidt Kümmel	6/3
Whisky Proprietary Brands	6/9	Benedictine	6/3
Vodka	6/3	Drambuie	6/3
Rum	6/3	Cointreau	6/3
Gin "London Square"	6/3	Gin Proprietary Brands	6/3

Whisky, Gin, Rum and Vodka are sold in two-fifths Gill Measures
Whisky and Gin are also available in one-fifth Gill Measures

BEERS 2/5
Bass "Blue Triangle"	Worthington	"Green Shield"	
Double Diamond	Whitbread	Guinness	Mackeson
Skol Lager	Harp Lager	Tuborg Lager	

Lager & Lime 2/10

CIDER 1/6
Bulmer's   Whiteway's

MINERALS

Schweppes:			
Ginger Beer	1/-	Pepsi-Cola	1/6
Tonic Water, Bitter Lemon	1/-	Vichy Célestins	2/6
Ginger Ale, Lemonade	1/-	Lime Juice Cordial	10d.
Sparkling Orange	1/-	Orange Squashes	10d.
Soda Water	1/-	Fruit Juices (assorted)	1/6

CIGARETTES
Wills Embassy	Player's Medium	Player's Gold Leaf Filter
Rothman's King Size Filter	Piccadilly Filter	
Sterling	Benson & Hedges King Size	

Leading Havana Cigars   Manikin Cigars   Wills Castella Panatellas
Churchman's Grande Short Panatellas

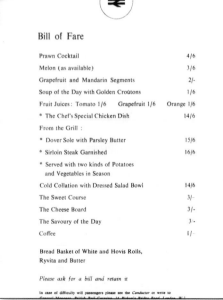

Bill of Fare

Prawn Cocktail	4/6
Melon (as available)	3/6
Grapefruit and Mandarin Segments	2/-
Soup of the Day with Golden Croûtons	1/6
Fruit Juices: Tomato 1/6 Grapefruit 1/6 Orange 1/6	
* The Chef's Special Chicken Dish	14/6

From the Grill :

* Dover Sole with Parsley Butter	15/6
* Sirloin Steak Garnished	16/6

* Served with two kinds of Potatoes
and Vegetables in Season

Cold Collation with Dressed Salad Bowl	14/6
The Sweet Course	3/-
The Cheese Board	3/-
The Savoury of the Day	3/-
Coffee	1/-

Bread Basket of White and Hovis Rolls,
Ryvita and Butter

Please ask for a bill and retain it

In case of difficulty will passengers please see the *Conductor* or write to
General Manager, British Rail Catering, 14 Bishop's Bridge Road, London, W.1

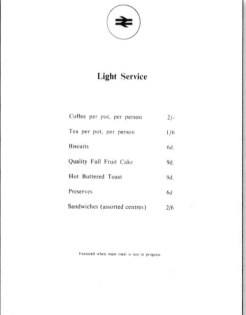

Light Service

Coffee per pot, per person	2/-
Tea per pot, per person	1/6
Biscuits	6d.
Quality Full Fruit Cake	9d.
Hot Buttered Toast	9d.
Preserves	6d
Sandwiches (assorted centres)	2/6

Featured when main meal is not in progress

The final view shows the up train on that last day. No D1924 is on the main line north of Waller's Ash. As a replacement for the loco-hauled 'Bournemouth Belle', the Southern Region had been offered the six-car multiple Blue Pullman sets, already redundant from the Midland Region after a life of just six years. Possibly in view of the poor riding reputation of these trains, the decision was taken to decline the offer, so the only regular Pullman train on the Southern Region was now the 'Brighton Belle', which would soldier on for a few more years. *Alistair Jeffery*

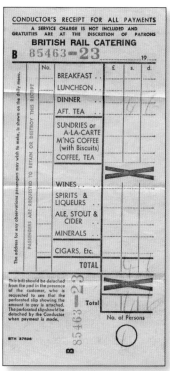

INDEX